THE BERMUDA TRIANGLE

MARYSA STORM

BLACK RABBIT BOOKS

Bolt Jr. is published by Black Rabbit Books
P.O. Box 3263, Mankato, Minnesota, 56002.
www.blackrabbitbooks.com
Copyright © 2020 Black Rabbit Books

Grant Gould, designer; Omay Ayres, photo researcher

Names: Storm, Marysa, author.
Title: The Bermuda Triangle / by Marysa Storm.
Description: Mankato, Minnesota : Bolt Jr. is published by
Black Rabbit Books, [2020] | Series: Bolt Jr.. a little bit
spooky | Audience: Ages: 6-8. | Audience: Grades:
K to Grade 3. | Includes bibliographical references and index.
Identifiers: LCCN 2019000896 (print) |
LCCN 2019010562 (ebook) | ISBN 9781623101848
(e-book) | ISBN 9781623101787 | (library binding) |
ISBN 9781644661161 (paperback)
Subjects: LCSH: Bermuda Triangle–Juvenile literature.
| Shipwrecks–Bermuda Triangle–Juvenile literature. |
Disappearances (Parapsychology)–Bermuda Triangle–
Juvenile literature. Classification: LCC G558 (ebook) |
LCC G558 .S76 2020 (print) | DDC 001.94–dc23
LC record available at https://lccn.loc.gov/2019000896

Printed in the United States. 5/19

Image Credits

Alamy: MasPix, 12; suriya silsaksom, 5; Dreamstime: Philcold,
8–9; militar.org.ua: Shipbucket, 19; Science Source: Victor Habbick
Visions, 6–7; Shutterstock: AC Rider, 22–23 (lightning); Andrew
Jalbert, 20–21; Andrey_Kuzmin, 8; Anna Andersson Fotografi, 7;
Bob Orsillo, 1; die Fotosynthese, Cover (plane); Dotted Yeti, 13;
e71lena, 11 (ship); KUROMO, 11 (bkgd); m.mphoto (boat, ocean);
Olga Popova, 10; Proskurina Yuliya, 3, 24; Pyty, 14–15; Rob Wilson,
4; Romolo Tavani, 18–19 (bkgd); Rorius, 14; S.Bachstroem, 16–17;
Sergey Nivens, Cover (bkgd); solar22, 21; Susanitah, 22–23 (ship)

Contents

CHAPTER 1

A Scary Story

Five planes fly over the ocean.

It's a calm day. But something's wrong.

The **compasses** aren't working.

The pilots are lost. They fly one

way. Then another. Then the planes

disappear. What happened?

compass: a tool used to
find direction

COMPARING BELIEVERS

About 59% of people believe the spot is safe.

Missing

The planes went missing in the Bermuda Triangle. It's a spot in the Atlantic Ocean. People talk about disappearances there. Some say something strange is happening. Others aren't so sure. They think it's all made-up.

About 41% of people believe the spot is unsafe.

Bermuda Triangle?

N25.8252 W80.1727

compasses not working

missing planes
and ships

N32,3242;W64,8413

storms

N18,3388;W64,0270

weird
lights

CHAPTER 2

Strange Happenings

People have talked about the spot for years. **Christopher Columbus** traveled there. He said he saw strange lights. In 1918, a big ship sailed there. It disappeared. So did everyone on board.

Christopher Columbus: an explorer during the late 1400s and early 1500s

What's Going On?

People say the spot isn't safe for many reasons. Some **blame** aliens. They say aliens take people. Others think monsters live there.

blame: to say someone or something is responsible for something

Where Is the Bermuda Triangle?

KEY

■ = Bermuda Triangle

Bermuda

Florida

Puerto Rico

CHAPTER 3

Studying the Stories

Some people say nothing's happening in that area. People travel through the spot every day. Nothing bad happens to them.

FACT

More than 20 planes have gone missing in the area.

The Real Reasons?

People have studied the stories.

They found that some never happened.

Storms caused some disappearances too.

But people can't explain all the

stories. Is something happening?

You decide.

Length of the Ship that Disappeared in 1918
almost **550** feet
(168 meters)

Bonus Facts

Some ships went missing without calling for help.

People have **made** movies about the spot.

The triangle was named in 1964.

It's also called the Devil's Triangle.

devil: an evil spirit

21

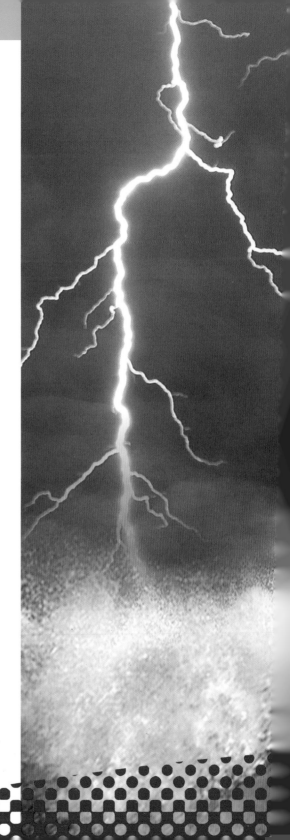

Loh-Hagan, Virginia. *Bermuda Triangle.* Urban Legends: Don't Read Alone! Ann Arbor, MI: Cherry Lake Publishing, 2018.

Polinsky, Paige V. *The Bermuda Triangle.* Investigating the Unexplained. Minneapolis: Bellwether Media, Inc., 2020.

Rauf, Don. *Mysterious Places.* Freaky Phenomena. Broomall, PA: Mason Crest, 2018.

Bermuda Triangle
kids.britannica.com/kids/article/
Bermuda-Triangle/598956

The Bermuda Triangle
www.coolkidfacts.com/the-bermuda-
triangle/

The Bermuda Triangle
www.sciencekids.co.nz/sciencefacts/
earth/bermudatriangle.html

GLOSSARY

blame (BLAYM)—to say someone or something is responsible for something

Christopher Columbus (KRIS-tuh-fer kuh-LUHM-buhs)—an explorer during the late 1400s and early 1500s

compass (KUM-pus)—a tool used to find direction

devil (DEV-uhl)—an evil spirit

INDEX